Come down, Zacchaeus!

Story by Penny Frank

Illustrated by John Haysom

THE LION
STORY BIBLE

43

OXFORD · BATAVIA · SYDNEY

The Bible tells us how God sent his Son Jesus to show us what God is like and how we can belong to God's kingdom. This story tells what happened when Jesus met a cheating tax collector called Zacchaeus, and the difference it made to his life. You can find the story in your own Bible, in Luke's Gospel, chapter 19.

Copyright © 1986 Lion Publishing

Published by
Lion Publishing plc
Sandy Lane West, Littlemore, Oxford, England
ISBN 0 85648 768 6
ISBN 0 7459 1788 7 (paperback)
Lion Publishing Corporation
1705 Hubbard Avenue, Batavia, Illinois 60510, USA
ISBN 0 85648 768 6
Albatross Books Pty Ltd
PO Box 320, Sutherland, NSW 2232, Australia
ISBN 0 86760 553 7
ISBN 0 7324 0108 9 (paperback)

First edition 1986, reprinted 1987, 1988 , 1992
Paperback edition 1989
Reprinted 1992

British Library Cataloguing in Publication Data

Frank, Penny
Come down, Zacchaeus! – (The Lion Story Bible; v. 43)
1. Zacchaeus – Juvenile literature
2. Bible stories, English – N.T. Luke
I. Title   II. Haysom, John
226'.40924   BS2520.Z3

ISBN 0-85648-768-6
ISBN 0-7459-1788-7 (paperback)

Library of Congress Cataloging in Publication Data

Frank, Penny.
Come down, Zacchaeus!
(The Lion Story Bible; 43)
1. Zacchaeus (Biblical character) –
Juvenile literature. [1. Zacchaeus
(Biblical character) 2. Bible stories –
N.T.] I. Haysom, John, ill. II. Title.
III. Series: Frank, Penny. Lion Story
Bible; 43.
BS2520.Z3F72 1986   226'.409505
85-24087
ISBN 0-85648-768-6
ISBN 0-7459-1788-7 (paperback)

Printed and bound in Slovenia

'Jesus is coming to Jericho today!' The
news spread quickly, from house to
house, through the villages.

Everyone wanted to see him. They all
hoped Jesus would speak to them, or
that he would heal someone. They
wanted to hear him tell a story.

No one was going to do much work
today, because Jesus was coming.

One of the people who lived in Jericho was a man called Zacchaeus. No one liked Zacchaeus. His job was to collect the tax which each person had to pay.

He was not an honest man. Often he made people pay more than they were supposed to.

'That's why he's so rich and we're so poor,' said the people.

Zacchaeus heard the news that Jesus was coming.

The people said, 'Jesus says that money does not matter in God's kingdom. The poor will come first and many rich people will be left outside.'

Zacchaeus didn't like the sound of that, but he wanted to see Jesus.

Zacchaeus was a very short man. He could not see over the shoulders of the people who stood waiting in the village street.

The children had climbed up on top of the walls to see.

There wasn't room for Zacchaeus anywhere.

Then Zacchaeus had an idea. There were trees in the village street. He quickly ran to the nearest tree and pulled himself up to the lowest branches.

Some of the children saw him climb into the tree.

They called out, 'Hey, look at old Zacchaeus. He's climbing up that tree!' and they laughed as his short legs disappeared among the leaves.

Then everyone stopped thinking about Zacchaeus, or anyone else.

They passed the news down the street that Jesus was coming.

Everyone leaned forward to be the first to see him. The children nearly toppled off the wall. They hung onto each other's arms.

They saw a group of people coming down the street. But everyone knew at once which man was Jesus. His face made them smile and feel glad when they saw him.

But why had Jesus stopped? Everyone was puzzled.

Jesus looked up into the tree. The people looked up too, and there was Zacchaeus peering down through the leaves.

'Zacchaeus,' Jesus called, laughing.
'Whatever are you doing up there?
Hurry and get down from that tree. I
want to spend today at your house.'

Zacchaeus was amazed as he scrambled down from the tree.

'How does Jesus know my name? How did he know I was there? He really seems to know me already.'

Zacchaeus kneeled down in the dusty road. The people couldn't believe what was happening.

'Please do come to my house,' they heard Zacchaeus say.

Zacchaeus hurried home to get things
ready. He sent his servants running to
do everything he told them. This was the
most important visitor he had ever had.

'We must offer him the best food we
have,' he told them.

But all the time Zacchaeus was thinking, 'Oh dear, Jesus is so good and he knows all about me. I could see that. He'll know about the money I've taken. He'll know just what a bad man I am when he sees this beautiful house.'

Jesus and his friends arrived, and they sat down to the meal. Zacchaeus felt worse and worse.

He saw the people going past the door.
They all peeped in and whispered,
'Look, Jesus is eating in the house of
Zacchaeus. Doesn't he know how
Zacchaeus gets his money?'

At last Zacchaeus could stand it no longer.

He looked at Jesus and spoke to him. Everyone stopped talking to listen to him.

'Sir, you know everything already. You know what a wicked man I've been. But I want to put things right. I'm going to give away half my money to those poor people outside. And the money I stole from them I will pay back four times over.'

'Well done, Zacchaeus,' said Jesus, smiling at him. 'That's the way to show you've come into God's kingdom.

'I came to this world,' Jesus went on, 'to seek and to save lost people. I am glad I found you today, Zacchaeus.'

The Lion Story Bible is made up of 52 individual stories for young readers, building up an understanding of the Bible as one story — God's story — a story for all time and all people.

The New Testament section (numbers 31–52) covers the life and teaching of God's Son, Jesus. The stories are about the people he met, what he did and what he said. Almost all we know about the life of Jesus is recorded in the four Gospels — Matthew, Mark, Luke and John. The word gospel means 'good news'.
 The last four stories in this section are about the first Christians, who started to tell others the 'good news', as Jesus had commanded them — a story which continues today all over the world.

The story of Zacchaeus comes from the New Testament, Luke's Gospel, chapter 19.
 God is not like us. He loves and cares about the nasty people as well as the nice ones. He wants everyone to be really sorry for the wrong things they have done, to put things right, and to follow him.
 Zacchaeus just wanted to take a look at Jesus. He did not expect Jesus to pay any attention to him. But, out of all the people in Jericho, Jesus chose to have dinner with Zacchaeus. He knew that Zacchaeus needed to be shown the way into God's kingdom. And once he had met Jesus, Zacchaeus became a new man.
 The next book in the series, number 44: *Mary, Martha and Lazarus*, is about three of Jesus' special friends — and a great miracle.